THE TALE OF THE TEE

BE KIND AND JUST BELIEVE

BK FULTON
JONATHAN BLANK

OWL PUBLISHING

5/25/22
To: Leon
Keep going ... until you reach all of your dreams!

THE TALE OF THE TEE™

The Tale of the Tee:
Be Kind and Just Believe
© 2020 by BK Fulton and Jonathan Blank

ISBN- 978-1-949929-47-8

All rights reserved. This book or any parts may not be reproduced in any form, electronic, mechanical, photocopy or otherwise, without written permission from the author. For permission requests, write to the publisher, addressed "Attention: Permissions Coordinator," at the address below.

Owl Publishing, LLC.

150 Parkview Heights Road, Ephrata PA 17522

717-925-7511

www.owlpublishinghouse.com

Cover Design and Interior Composition by Rachel Loughlin
rachelloughlin.com
Photos: page 48, 37 bottom (2,3), 38 bottom (2), 39 bottom (2)

Editing by E. Ce Miller
seventhsliterary.com

Photos by Queon "Q" Martin
Page 6, 8, 9, 10, 11, 35, 36-37, 37 bottom (1), 38-39, 38 bottom (1), 39 bottom (1), 40-41, 52-53, 58-59

Published in the United States of America

TABLE OF CONTENTS

Preface	6
Introduction	8
BK Fulton's VCU da Vinci Center Graduation Address: Remembering Those on the Margins	16
1 Angry Black Man	32
The Divine Puzzle of Life as Seen by a Native Son of Virginia	40
Dr. George Franklin Grant	50
Confederate Symbols Must Go at Freeman High School	53
JB's remarks at the McGuireWoods Town Hall	57
Conclusion	60
About BK Fulton	62
About Jonathan Blank	63

DEDICATION

*This book is dedicated to my Angel Network
(you know who you are).
Thank you for the support and continuous uplift as we
traverse this beautiful journey called* **Life.**

BK FULTON

---

*This book is dedicated to Dr. George Grant and
those on the margins whose stories we have too long
ignored, and to BK for taking me on this journey.*

JONATHAN T. BLANK

PREFACE

WITH ALL THE UNREST IN THE NATION AND ACROSS THE WORLD RIGHT NOW, CLEARLY CHANGE IS NEEDED.

In an oddly divine way, during this time of uncertainty and upheaval, my wife Jackie shared some of my work—specifically, the release of our critically acclaimed and award-winning film **1 Angry Black Man** and a commencement speech I gave for Virginia Commonwealth University's da Vinci Center that went mini-viral—with Jonathan Blank, a colleague and partner at her law firm. That simple act of sharing started an e-mail chain between myself and Jonathan, who I did not know well at the time. The honest and heartfelt exchanges led to us both keeping a particular memento with us at all times: a golf tee.

Jonathan originally reached out to Jackie after he saw an article in a local paper about her and two other partners from the firm—Tracy Walker and Sam Tarry—cleaning the Oliver Hill historical marker, which recently had been vandalized. Hill was one of the lawyers who conceived and won the <u>Brown v. Board of Education</u> case in 1954. Jackie and her colleagues were pictured cleaning the sign and the Richmond Times-Dispatch picked up the story.

Jonathan and I became pen pals during the course of these events, writing long missives back and forth. Our correspondence is a testament to truth and the opportunity for conversation and connection that this current moment in history affords us. I pray that we are all brave enough to take advantage of this historic ripple in time. What you are about to read captures verbatim, "The Tale of the Tee."

June 18, 2020

INTRODUCTION

BK FULTON • JONATHAN BLANK

On May 25, 2020, African-American truck driver and security guard George Floyd was murdered by police during an arrest outside a Minneapolis, Minnesota convenience store. His death ignited a series of protests against police violence toward Black people in the United States and around the world. The protests were largely supported by Black Lives Matter, a nonviolent activist movement founded in 2013 after the acquittal of George Zimmerman, who shot to death African-American teen Trayvon Martin in 2012.

The protests began in Minneapolis on May 26 and quickly spread across all 50 states and internationally. Almost a month later the marches, protests, and other acts of strategic civil disobedience were still ongoing nationwide—including in Richmond, Virginia, the so-called "Capital of the Confederacy" due to Jefferson Davis locating his "presidential" residence there from August 1861 until April 1865.

RICHMOND ALSO HAD BECOME A FLASHPOINT FOR PROTESTERS DUE TO THE LOCATION OF SEVERAL ENORMOUS MONUMENTS PAYING HOMAGE TO CONFEDERATE GENERALS AND PLACED IN THE GEOGRAPHIC CENTER OF VIRGINIA'S CAPITAL CITY.

Despite the nonviolent mission of Black Lives Matter, some protests quickly turned destructive. Acts of looting, rioting, and arson often were committed by direct opponents of Black Lives Matter, those trying to distract media attention from the movement, and some misdirected protestors themselves. Confederate monuments across the United States were covered in graffiti, while some protestors attempted to topple others. Simultaneously, monuments to Union leaders who were slave owners themselves and memorials to Civil Rights activists and leaders in the African-American community also were defaced.

This included the historical marker honoring Civil Rights attorney Oliver Hill Sr., located on East Main Street outside the Lewis F. Powell Jr. U.S. Courthouse in Richmond.

On the morning of June 9, Richmond attorney Jacquelyn E. Stone and two of her colleagues from the McGuireWoods law firm were noticed by a passerby while cleaning spray paint off the Oliver Hill marker by hand. The marker had just been unveiled on Main Street that February, when the City of Richmond installed it to honor Oliver Hill Sr., a man who had practiced law for almost 60 years, worked on the [Brown v. Board of Education](#) case that was instrumental in leading the movement to desegregate schools nationwide and was awarded the Presidential Medal of Freedom by President Bill Clinton in 1997.

06.09.2020

Stone, whose husband is a former Verizon Communications President turned author and film producer —BK Fulton—knew Hill personally. He had been a friend and mentor to her father, Williamsburg attorney and judge, the Honorable William T. Stone—the first black judge in Virginia. Doing what was right and what was just came naturally to Stone and her colleagues, who didn't want to pass by a graffiti-covered plaque dishonoring the legacy of a Civil Rights leader and pioneer in the law.

A few days later, Stone and her colleagues were contacted by local media.

On June 12, the *Richmond Times-Dispatch* ran an article by reporter Mike Barber about the local attorneys cleaning the Oliver Hill plaque. The story, *Richmond Attorneys Clean Vandalized Plaque Honoring Civil Rights Pioneer*, was subsequently picked up by local and national media, garnering the attention of Stone, Tarry, and Walker's colleagues at McGuireWoods.

06.12.2020

THE FOLLOWING EXCHANGE IS WHAT TRANSPIRED FROM THAT INITIAL ACT OF GOODWILL.

THE TALE OF THE TEE

06.14.2020

FROM: JONATHAN T. BLANK

Sent: Sunday, June 14, 2020 10:26 AM
To: Stone, Jacquelyn E.

Thank you for cleaning the Oliver Hill marker. The article made me proud to be your friend and partner.

I have always felt that small acts have ripple effects.

I hope you are staying well.

Jonathan T. Blank

Partner
McGuireWoods LLP

HAVE RIPPLE EFFECTS

FROM: JACQUELYN E. STONE

Sent: Sunday, June 14, 2020 10:59 AM
To: Blank, Jonathan T.

Thank you for your message and kind comments. Hope you and your family are well. We are doing fine. In fact, BK is busier than ever. He was scheduled to give the commencement speech to this year's graduating class of the VCU da Vinci Center. Since the commencement was postponed, BK worked with the school to deliver their first ever virtual commencement address, which is available for viewing online. I've included a link below. Please feel free to share. Take care!

Jackie

Jacquelyn E. Stone
Partner
McGuireWoods LLP

BK FULTON'S VCU DA VINCI CENTER GRADUATION ADDRESS:
REMEMBERING THOSE ON THE MARGINS

It's an honor and a privilege to be here today. I feel I am in great company with the next generation of innovators from our community.

I BELIEVE YOU WILL CHANGE THE WORLD.

I have been thinking of what I might say to you that would be of some value. You all are so smart, and I'm just a film and technology guy. I know that whatever I say, I better not take too long. Your family is in quarantine and they long to hold you close before you go off to change the world. And you probably have some Zoom partying or Tik Toking to do—is that right? You all have a life. All of that is good.

I'm going to need your help to get through this. Yes, one more class participation session and you're all done.

MY FOCUS THIS MORNING IS ON THE PEOPLE ON THE MARGINS – THE 95% OF THE WORLD WHO DON'T YET KNOW HOW GREAT THEY ARE. IF YOU TAKE ANYTHING FROM MY ADDRESS TODAY, PLEASE TAKE THIS: ALWAYS REMEMBER THOSE ON THE MARGINS.

You may be asking why would I implore you to remember those on the margins: the poor, people with disabilities, women, minorities, the undereducated, and people outside the economic mainstream. Let me demonstrate, with your assistance.

By show of hands, did anyone turn on a light in your home last night or this morning? Did anyone pass a red, yellow, or green signal light on your way to get food or check in on a loved one? (I do hope you stopped at the red light.) How many of you sent a letter in the mail this week? Does anyone here have a home security system?

Keep your hands up.

Did anyone recently go to the grocery store for fresh produce? Instacart people—that means you too. Did anyone turn on a heater in the winter months? Did anyone use a cell phone in the past twenty-four hours? Do you think medical breakthroughs like blood plasma or open-heart surgery are important to humanity?

Okay, that's it. Thank you for your participation. You all get an A+.

I think you know where I'm going with this: all of the things I just mentioned were created by people on the margins.

LET ME ILLUMINATE JUST A FEW OF THEM.

The mailbox, or "street letter box" as it was called in 1891, was invented by **Philip B. Downing**. Before his invention, people with mail had to go to the post office to drop off letters and packages. Once the mailbox was invented, drop offs could happen at the local street letter box.

 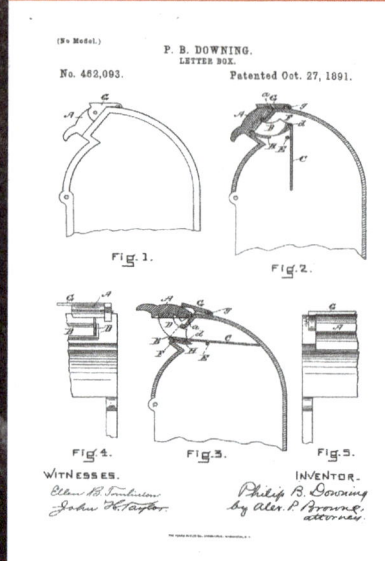

Refrigerated trucks were invented by **Frederick McKinley Jones** in the 1940s. His invention allowed produce in grocery stores to stay fresh.

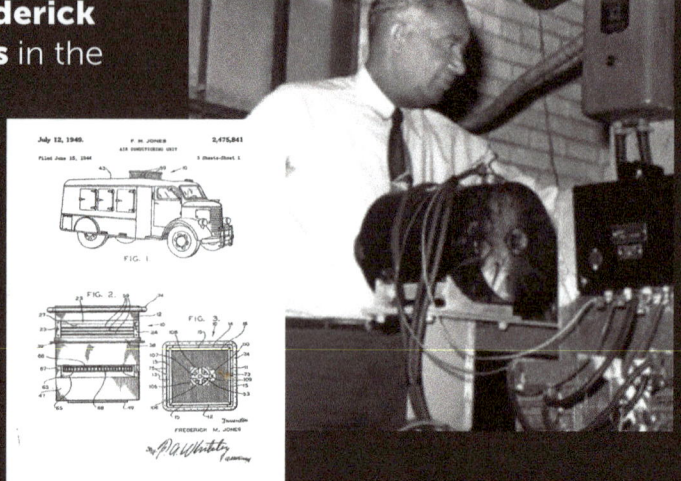

The signal traffic light was invented by **Garrett Morgan** in 1923, after he saw a terrible carriage accident. He later sold the patent rights to General Electric for $40,000.

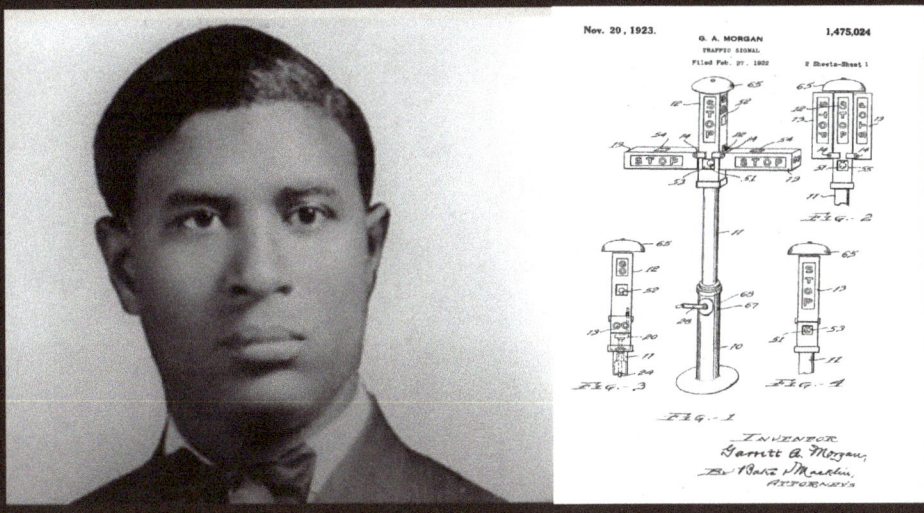

 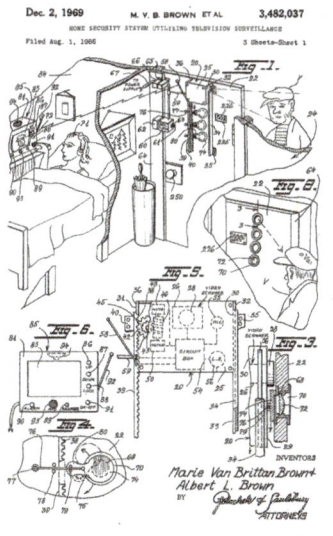

Marie Van Brittan Brown invented the home security system in 1969, in response to high incidents of crime in her Queens neighborhood. Her original design included a video camera. Sound familiar? (Can you say Ring Doorbell?)

Alice H. Parker invented the natural heating furnace in 1919. Today's forced-air heating systems are modeled after Ms. Parker's design.

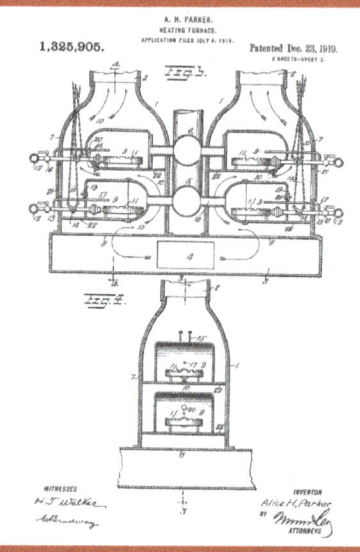

In the 1970s, **Shirley Ann Jackson**—the first Black woman to receive a PhD from MIT—led the team that developed the touchtone phone, caller ID, and call waiting.

CAN YOU HEAR ME NOW?

BK FULTON • JONATHAN BLANK

Dr. Gladys West invented the GPS, also known as the Global Positioning System, and was inducted into the Space and Missile Pioneers Hall of Fame in 2018 by the United States Air Force.

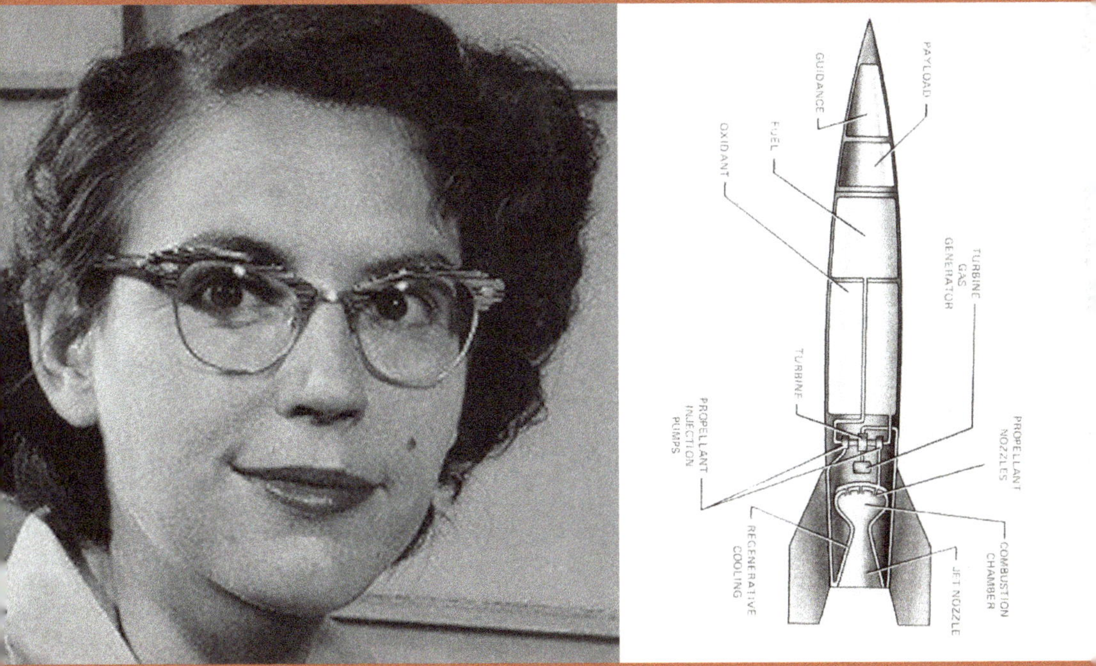

Mary Sherman Morgan—aka "the rocket girl"—was a petite woman from North Dakota. She helped to create rocket fuel. Her fuel mixture allowed America to win the Space Race.

THE TALE OF THE TEE

We cannot talk about space without a thankful nod to **Ms. Katherine Johnson**, who passed earlier this year at the age of 101. Some of her colleagues at NASA thought she was the maid when, in fact, she was a brilliant mathematician—called a "human computer." She calculated complex orbital trajectories by hand. She was memorialized in the Hollywood film *Hidden Figures*. Astronaut John Glenn trusted her calculations more than he did the mechanical computers.

BK FULTON • JONATHAN BLANK

Let's not forget "Amazing Grace" — **Ms. Grace Hopper**—who invented the first compiler that allowed computers to talk to each other. She also co-invented COBOL, the first commercial programming language widely used in government and business. She was told that computers only did math. That was true, until it wasn't. Grace developed the system that turned common English words into machine code. Thanks to pioneers like Grace, we're now racing down the roads of artificial intelligence, augmented reality, and quantum-level computing. Our computers can now order groceries, tell us jokes, and one day they may even do a commencement address.

Last, but not least, **Lewis Howard Latimer** added the carbon filament to Thomas Edison's light bulb. Edison originally used paper filaments that burned out quickly. The Latimer improvement gives us the bulbs we use to this day. Latimer also wrote the first book on incandescence and went on to draft the patent drawings and notes for the telephone. He sold his work to a company that would become General Electric. Lewis Latimer also supervised the installation of public electric lights throughout New York, Philadelphia, Montreal, and London. He was on the margins. His parents were former slaves in Virginia who escaped north in search of a better life.

THE TALE OF THE TEE

THINK ABOUT THE LIKELIHOOD OF A PERSON WHO WAS NOT EVEN SUPPOSED TO LEARN TO READ INVENTING THE FILAMENT FOR THE LIGHT BULB AND DRAWING THE PATENT FILING FOR THE TELEPHONE.

Let that sink in.

There are thousands of remarkable stories like this that have been kept from us. I pray that God forgives us for focusing more on lost causes than on finding needed cures. It's as if we're looking up for ideas and only choosing to see half the sky. The people on the margins should not be made invisible.

WHAT CAN WE LEARN FROM THESE PEOPLE WHO CHANGED THE WORLD FOR THE BETTER, IN SPITE OF THE OBSTACLES? WHAT THEIR WORK TELLS ME IS THAT **THE REAL GENIUS IN THE WORLD IS IN RECOGNIZING THE GENIUS IN OTHERS.**

My hypothesis is that we all have the capacity to be great. God distributes talent generously throughout our species, and all of us get to have the life we're willing to work for. It is in our naked self-interest to invest in everyone: every girl and every boy on the planet, because we have no idea where the cure for ALS is coming from. We have no idea where the cure for cancer is coming from. We have no idea where the cure for Alzheimer's is coming from. What we do know for sure is that the cures that will help your family and mine are randomly distributed somewhere out there in the world. What we do know for sure is that the person with the cure we need right now might just be listening to this message. What we do know for sure is that the antidote for all that ails us is you.

I CHALLENGE YOU TO DECIDE TO BE GREAT—because if a person on the margins can achieve at the highest levels, what is our excuse for dabbling in mediocrity? Before I invented anything, before writing my eighth book, before my AR firm won the top seven figure prize for the 2020 Global 5G Challenge, before I ran a multi-billion dollar company for Verizon with over 40,000 employees, before I made my first movie with Lionsgate,

I WAS A PERSON ON THE MARGINS.

THE TALE OF THE TEE

I almost flunked out of engineering school. It was reading about people like Mr. Latimer that changed my life. I realized that if he could change the world at the time he was alive, with very few resources and limited support, I could change my trajectory if I applied myself.

THE STORIES OF SUCCESS AND INNOVATION HELPED ME TO STOP SEEING THE WORLD THROUGH A PRISM OF SORROWS.

INSTEAD, I LEARNED TO LOOK AT THE WORLD THROUGH THE LENS OF ACHIEVEMENT.

This shift in my worldview has made all the difference. Life is a journey. When we learn better we must do better.

WE DO NOT GET TO CHOOSE WHERE WE START, BUT WE DO GET TO CHOOSE WHERE WE END UP.

I am thankful for all those that sacrificed—every ethnicity and every gender—to show us what it means to be human, and how the pursuit of excellence allows us to pay forward the gift of our very existence.

Complaining about tough times, complaining about what we don't have, blaming everyone else for what we have failed to do as people is an inadequate contribution to the future of our success. Yes, I chair seven companies, and I still read every day, and at times work into the wee hours of the morning. When the curious ask why I work so much as a retired person, and why I send emails at 3 and 4 a.m., I tell them that "I work while they sleep so I can live like they dream."

> INNOVATORS ARE CURIOUS PEOPLE.
> **WE SEEK UNDERSTANDING AS WE FIND OUR PLACE IN THE WORLD.**
> I HAVE LEARNED TO SET ASIDE EXCUSES.
> I EXIST TO FIND THE OPPORTUNITIES IN LIFE THAT BRING ME JOY.

What I have also learned is that the world is full of opportunities, and the best innovators know how to create opportunities as well. You are innovators.

"START WHERE YOU ARE. USE WHAT YOU HAVE. DO WHAT YOU CAN."

Arthur Ashe said that.

It's good advice.

Did you know that Steven Spielberg has dyslexia? So does Cher, Tim Tebow, Keira Knightley, Whoopi Goldberg, Adam Leipzig, Daniel Radcliffe, and Anderson Cooper. Albert Einstein, JFK, George Washington, and even Leonardo da Vinci also had dyslexia. Did you know that Justin Timberlake has ADHD? So does Lisa Ling.

What's my point?

THESE AILMENTS DID NOT HOLD ANY OF THESE TALENTED HUMAN BEINGS BACK FROM BECOMING THE BEST VERSION OF THEMSELVES. IN FACT, ONE COULD ARGUE THAT THEY LEARNED TO USE THEIR CHALLENGES TO SOAR.

CONSIDER THIS: PEOPLE WHO ARE DYSLEXIC HAVE AN EXTRAORDINARY ABILITY TO SOLVE PROBLEMS. In fact, according to professor Julie Logan, professor of entrepreneurship at the Cass Business School in London, 35% of the entrepreneurs she surveyed across the United States identified themselves as dyslexic. **Her study concluded that dyslexics were more likely than non-dyslexics to delegate authority, excel in oral communication and problem solving, and were twice as likely to own two or more businesses.**

I think I may be a little bit dyslexic—and I'm okay with that. My wife may say that I'm completely dyslexic, and she's okay with that. (Thank you, honey.)

I FIND IT INTERESTING THAT THE PEOPLE WHO GIVE THE MOST ARE OFTEN THE PEOPLE WHO HAVE THE LEAST.

I'm reminded of a picture of Albert Einstein that hangs in my office. It's an image of the great scientist giving a private lecture to a small class of African-American men at Lincoln University, an HBCU. The esteemed scientist rarely gave guest lectures, so I was puzzled why he regularly agreed to give lectures to these young men on the margins. A few months ago, the president of Norfolk State University, where I serve on the board of trustees, shared a Washington Post article with me that made everything more clear. You see, during World War II German Jews were having difficulty getting visas into the United States.

There was a law called the Public Charge Policy that required immigrants to prove they would not become a burden on the nation before they were allowed in. The prevailing US policy was an effective death sentence for German Jews.

It turned out that HBCUs—not the more prestigious universities or the US government—gave jobs to Jewish scholars to help them make their way to safety in the United States and away from the Holocaust.

EINSTEIN WAS A GERMAN JEW. HE KNEW THIS HISTORY AND RESPECTED THE SACRIFICE AND COURAGE OF THE HBCUS TO HELP HIS PEOPLE ON THE MARGINS. MANY LIVES WERE SAVED BECAUSE OF THIS COURAGE. EINSTEIN WAS SIMPLY PAYING FORWARD THE KINDNESS. HE DID NOT FORGET THOSE ON THE MARGINS.

Let me close with Leonardo da Vinci. The man for whom your program is named was also a person on the margins. I already told you he had dyslexia. Did you also know that he was born out of wedlock? That's right—illegitimate. Did you know his orphaned mother was no more than sixteen years old when she gave birth to him? He was the oldest of twelve siblings. Did you know that he was born impoverished and had no formal education? He was also jailed briefly because some did not agree with his choice of life companions. Yes, he loved those on the margins.

From these humble beginnings, da Vinci became a great painter and one of the world's great minds—considered a bona fide polymath, or multi-talented genius and Renaissance man. His *Mona Lisa* is the most recognized portrait in the world. *The Last Supper* is the most reproduced religious painting of all time. And his *Salvator Mundi* is the most expensive painting ever sold at public auction. It was purchased in 2017 for almost $500 million. This year for the first time, the Louvre in Paris opened for 24 hours on a weekend so more visitors could see the final days of the otherwise sold-out da Vinci exhibit. The exhibit opened on October 24, 2019 to celebrate the 500th anniversary of da Vinci's death. The exhibit of drawings and paintings shattered the museum's attendance record, with over 1 million visitors stopping by to see the collection of works by the great Renaissance man.

So what's the point of all this meandering through history? Let me tell you:

IF YOU THINK LIGHTS ARE IMPORTANT, IF YOU THINK FRESH PRODUCE IS IMPORTANT, IF YOU THINK GETTING YOUR MAIL OR HAVING GPS IS IMPORTANT, IF YOU THINK OPEN-HEART SURGERY IS IMPORTANT, IF YOU THINK ART IS IMPORTANT, IF YOU THINK YOUR PHONE, ROCKET FUEL, COMPUTERS, AND SPACE FLIGHT ARE AMONG THE IMPORTANT CONTRIBUTIONS TO THE HISTORY OF HUMANITY, KNOW THAT ALL OF THESE THINGS WERE CREATED BY PEOPLE ON THE MARGINS.

Accordingly, I respectfully ask that when you leave this place today—and for the rest of your lives—pay the lessons you have learned here forward. Choose to be excellent. And remember those on the margins.

Congratulations da Vinci class of 2020. You have earned this graduation and no one can take that away. Become the change you seek. Thank you.

BK FULTON
May 8, 2020

FROM: JACQUELYN E. STONE

Sent: Sunday, June 14, 2020 11:02 AM
To: Blank, Jonathan T.
Subject: BK's film

I also wanted to share that the Boston Globe's Pulitzer Prize finalist for criticism—Ty Burr—reviewed BK's film *1 Angry Black Man*, which is available NOW On-demand and DVD everywhere. Attached below are other reviews from the national press. See additional details and information at www.soulidifly.com.

Jacquelyn E. Stone
Partner
McGuireWoods LLP

Trailer - https://www.soulidifly.com/1-angry-black-man-1

★★★☆

3 out of 4 stars

"Lessons extend very far beyond the classroom…"

Pulitzer Prize Finalist Film Critic - Ty Burr

IN '1 ANGRY BLACK MAN,' LESSONS THAT EXTEND VERY FAR BEYOND THE CLASSROOM

More a dramatized seminar than a movie in the traditional sense, "1 Angry Black Man" nevertheless arrives on video streaming platforms at the best worst possible time. Black men lie murdered by police, cities are burning, the country's racial injustices have never been plainer to see even by whites. Menelek Lumumba's film takes place in academia, over the course of one Black Literature college class with a diverse array of students, but over the course of its 90-plus minutes, the roar of unrest becomes deafening.

EXCERPT BY TY BURR, BOSTON GLOBE.COM
June 3, 2020 (3 out of 4 stars)

THE TALE OF THE TEE

OFFICIAL SELECTION BlackStar Film Festival 2018 | **OFFICIAL SELECTION** BronzeLens Film Festival 2018 | **OFFICIAL SELECTION** Urbanworld Film Festival 2018 | **OFFICIAL SELECTION** AFIKANA Film Festival 2018

Award-Winning

"Black Girl Nerds calls the film 'Impactful,' singling out its 'cerebral discussions…'"

The Washington Post

"A brilliant discourse on black literature juxtaposed with systemic racial oppression."

MEDIA & ENTERTAINMENT

"1 Angry Black Man is more than its title."

HOUSTON ⭑ CHRONICLE

"Is *1 Angry Black Man* the most important film opening online this week? It might be."

BOSTON Herald

'1 ANGRY BLACK MAN' A STELLAR DEBUT FOR OUR TIMES

Is "*1 Angry Black Man*" the most important film opening online this week? It might be. The film begins with its African-American protagonist Mike (a very good Keith Stone), sitting handcuffed in a police station in Maine, where he attends fictional Frost University. Mike is from Chicago, or as the police officer puts it, "a street kid from Chicago coming to Maine." He has been charged with assault by the intoxicated young white woman he walked to her room the night before. It's a "he-said, she said" case. He said he was trying to protect her. Guess whose odds are not very good?

In this age of #MeToo and #BelieveAllWomen, this is a tricky move on the part of writer-director and Denver, Colo., native Menelek Lumumba, making his impressive debut. People in the woke community might not like this angle. But I believe they should reread "To Kill a Mockingbird" before they complain. Suddenly, Mike is set free. All charges dropped. He's relieved. But how could this college student go from "Chicago street kid" headed for prison to college kid once again?

America is the resounding answer this film gives us. What happens next is unique in my experience as a film critic.

EXCERPT BY JAMES VERNIERE, BOSTON HERALD
June 5, 2020 (B+)

FROM: JONATHAN T. BLANK

Sent: Sunday, June 14, 2020 3:11 PM
To: Stone, Jacquelyn E.
Subject: RE:

Very powerful.

Please tell him the same.

I had never heard many of those stories including the Einstein HBCU story.

Post-MW town hall, we should be committed to keeping the conversation going forever.

BK would be a great presenter to MW and not just the attorneys.

> One day, school curriculum will focus on the stories of those on the margins.
>
> **BUT THEY DO NOT DO SO NOW.**
>
> I never heard them.

BK's commencement speech is as necessary for the MW family and others as it was for the graduates.

As for me, all is well. I had a crazy health scare in early to mid-March but survived to tell the story. It was not COVID as far as we know. I was hospitalized in Orlando while doing deposition prep with pulmonary embolism in right and left lungs. I am fine now (and pretty much a week later), but it was scary. Every day, I hug the twins and Susan and thankful that I got more time. Mom and Dad are also well and just left a social distance lunch at my house. Look forward to seeing you in person. Stay well.

Jonathan T. Blank
McGuireWoods LLP

FROM: JACQUELYN E. STONE

Sent: Sunday, June 14, 2020 3:28 PM
To: Blank, Jonathan T.
Cc: 'BK' <bkfulton@aol.com>
Subject: RE:

Thanks so much for your message. I had no idea you had been sick and am very pleased to hear you are doing better. Please take care of yourself and give your family our warmest regards.

BK&J

Jacquelyn E. Stone
Partner
McGuireWoods LLP

FROM: BK FULTON

Sent: Sunday, June 14, 2020
3:35 PM
To: Stone, Jacquelyn E.
Cc: Blank, Jonathan T.
Subject: Re:

Jonathan,

Thank you for the kudos and we are also glad that you got more time. Too often humans fail to do what they are supposed to do with their quality time remaining ("QTR"). You have a new lease on life and likely a whole new appreciation for how fragile it is. I can't wait to see and experience all the great things you will do with your QTR. Best.

BK

FROM: JONATHAN T. BLANK

On Jun 14, 2020, at 3:54 PM,

Thanks BK. Your QTR assessment is spot on.

Looking forward to a pandemic loosening (ending is too far off) QTR drink.

In the meantime, *1 Angry Black Man* is next on the list for Susan and me.

Jonathan T. Blank

McGuireWoods LLP

FROM: **BK FULTON**

Sent: Sunday, June 14, 2020 6:15 PM
To: Blank, Jonathan T.
Cc: Stone, Jacquelyn E.
Subject: Re:

Sounds fabulous! Let me know what you think of *1 Angry Black Man*. I appear to have stirred up a bit of a heady conversation on Bacon's Rebellion today. I wrote the op-ed on Saturday afternoon and it was published this morning. Enjoy!

BK

THE TALE OF THE TEE

THE DIVINE PUZZLE OF LIFE
AS SEEN BY A NATIVE SON OF VIRGINIA

ORIGINALLY PUBLISHED ON:
https://www.baconsrebellion.com/

OUR NATION HAS NOT YET FULLY ADDRESSED ITS ORIGINAL SIN . . . THE SAVAGE INSTITUTION OF SLAVERY. THE RESIDUE OF INEQUALITY STILL PERMEATES OUR SHORES AND INFECTS THE GLOBE AS A PANDEMIC OF THE MIND.

Despite our scientific similarities (we are more alike than different), when it comes to power — both its use and restraint — IN 2020 WE STILL RUN INTO A REFRAIN OF **WHITE RESISTANCE** AND THE ODDITY OF **WHITE FRAILTY.**

These two pillars of privilege shape a misinformed, yet powerful worldview of the pecking order of humanity that we all experience in contemporary America and beyond.

Over the course of 50+ years of being American and Virginian, I have learned that we are all simply human beings sharing the same rock. I try to teach my children and friends who will listen that we are all cousins trying to find our way home. I also teach my sons that while they should enjoy the same rights and privileges as others, the reality is that the sickness created by a culture that would rather teach lies about Christopher Columbus than acknowledge truths about Lewis H. Latimer (the Virginian son of runaway slaves who invented the filament for the present-day light bulb), means they exist in a world that does not always protect the value of their humanity.

> A CULTURE THAT OVERPLAYS **WHITE CONTRIBUTIONS** AND UNDERPLAYS THE CONTRIBUTIONS OF **PEOPLE OF COLOR** WILL UNDERPLAY THE IMPORTANCE OF **WHO THEY ARE** AS YOUNG BLACK MEN.

The educational and political systems of our Land, formal and informal, have too often perpetuated a Eurocentric indoctrination of humanity versus teaching critical thinking. It is up to civil society to close the gap between the two. This is where the "truth" lives … in the gap.

HOW I WISH WE COULD SEE OURSELVES AS PART OF A DIVINE PUZZLE OF LIFE. IN THIS PUZZLE, WE ARE ALL ESSENTIAL PIECES. OUR RESPECTIVE CONTRIBUTIONS ARE IMPORTANT AND UNIQUE TO THE PUZZLE.

WE ALL ADD VALUE.

What is clear with this framing of life, is that a person has to know who he or she is so that they know where they fit in the puzzle. It is critically important to know your place in the world before you can determine what you must do in the world. You can't know your place unless you know who you are. In America, we pretend that African-American history started in Virginia in 1619. We tell every child in school this fiction. We tell them how Christopher Columbus discovered America. He did not. We leave out of the American story almost every important contribution from non-whites and go further to erect monuments and give platitudes for characters in our history who in fact tried to tear up our more perfect union and subjugate black men and women to the horrors of chattel slavery.

Our schools do not teach us that when black men and women played by the rules and built up banks, and schools, and self-sufficient communities like in Tulsa, Oklahoma, those cities were literally bombed and burned to the ground by angry whites, often for the trumped up charge of an offense against a white woman. If we only told the truth, we could mitigate these atrocities and tragic mishaps of humanity and press on to a world where each citizen (each piece in the divine puzzle) could develop without the pathology of indoctrination and contribute beyond the basic instinct to survive. When we all come into the full knowledge of who we are, we will know where we fit in the divine puzzle of life.

IS IT TOO EARLY IN 2020 TO BE HONEST IN AMERICA? IS WHITE FRAILTY SO ENTRENCHED IN OUR WHITE BROTHERS' AND SISTERS' MINDS THAT THEY CAN'T HANDLE THE TRUTH?

I THINK NOT.

The streets of America and other cities around the world are filled with protesters of all ethnicities precisely because we have all been lied to. The lynching of George Floyd and the murder of many other innocents have brought us to a tipping point. For the sake of our sons and daughters, I hope things will never be the same.

IT'S TIME FOR THE TRUTH, AMERICA.

AS WE EMERGE FROM THIS GLOBAL PANDEMIC, MAY WE ALSO EMERGE FROM THE SYSTEMIC PANDEMICS OF HATRED AND FEAR FUELED BY THE CONTAGIOUS PEDAGOGY OF WHITE SUPREMACY.

IT IS TIME FOR REAL CHANGE. THE TRUTH WILL SET US FREE.

BK's op-ed was published on Sunday, June 14th in a local e-zine and attracted 39 comments that covered all political persuasions and ideas on BK's musings. Most were favorable. The op-ed was later picked up by Maria Shriver's Sunday Paper – *Voices Above the Noise* – and published to a national audience on June 17th. In reaction to one of the comments to the op-ed, BK mentioned that common history like George Franklin Grant's invention of the golf tee is a part of American history that never gets taught broadly to students in the US.

> **THESE CHOICES OF WHAT TO INCLUDE IN HISTORY AND WHAT NOT TO INCLUDE IMPACT STUDENTS' BELIEF ABOUT WHO THEY ARE AND WHAT PEOPLE LIKE THEM ARE CAPABLE OF.**

BK noted that we underplay the contributions of people of color and overplay contributions of whites. He says this problem feeds white supremacist indoctrination in our society and should be corrected.

FROM: JONATHAN T. BLANK

Sent: Jun 14, 2020 at 9:14 PM
To: BK

1. Thank you for sharing.

YOUR BACON'S REBELLION PIECE WAS VERY SIMILAR TO PART OF A CONVERSATION I WAS HAVING WITH ONE OF MY HIGH SCHOOL CLASSMATES THIS WEEK. IT WAS IN THE CONTEXT OF WHY HENRICO COUNTY SCHOOLS AND STUDENTS FELT SO COMFORTABLE WITH CONFEDERATE SYMBOLS OVER THE PAST 50 YEARS. A THESIS WAS THE ABSENCE OF AFRICAN-AMERICAN CURRICULUM AND SUGARCOATED TEACHINGS OF THE CIVIL WAR.

The posts and your response also fascinated me.

2. As a golf lover, I had no idea about George Franklin Grant or his Jackie and Susan-like Harvard pedigree.

Jonathan T. Blank
McGuireWoods LLP

FROM: BK FULTON

Sent: Jun 14, 2020, at 10:11 PM
To: Blank, Jonathan T.

Thanks for sharing. I look forward to chatting. I find that people are ostensibly comfortable with many things they should not be. Rarely are they asked what they are actually thinking, so we don't get their validated point of view. Indoctrination creates a reward for reciting the "right" fact (even if it's a false fact).

Why are most people comfortable with the myth of Christopher Columbus? He never made it to the continental United States. The comfort lies in the perpetuation of the lie. You hear it enough and you just go with it. You forget that you have been lied to. It only irritates when it becomes a challenge to your worldview. The fact that his "discovery" is fiction, becomes one of many inconvenient truths.

The education systems in our nation were never meant to create leaders in children of color. That is why there are so few examples of our many contributions. The education systems in our country were also designed to erase white aggression against innocent people and victims. Playing by the rules was not valued unless they were the rules that kept the majority on top; at all costs.

OUR HISTORY IS BOTH SORDID AND IN SOME PLACES GLORIOUS. YESTERDAY'S ABOLITIONIST IS TODAY'S PROGRESSIVE. I love the white folk that helped the enslaved to find freedom. Those people are some of my heroes because they were pioneers of lifting up humanity at all costs. It gives me chills thinking about those white people. Those are MY people. You are one of those people and in a turn of a phrase, we are no longer black or white; **WE ARE SIMPLY BROTHERS SHARING THE SAME ROCK, THE SAME AIR, AND THE SAME LAND . . . UNDER ONE GOD. IT'S NOT THAT HEAVY UNLESS WE CHOOSE TO MAKE IT SO.**

BK

06.15.2020

The conversation continues into the following day, with both men discovering that not only had the idea of truth increasingly been on their minds as the national unrest continued, but that each had published articles on truth in the same week they began corresponding. Fulton's *The Divine Puzzle of Life as Seen by a Native Son of Virginia*, is reproduced above. Blank's *Letter to the Editor, Confederate symbols must go at Freeman High School*, can be found in later correspondence below.

FROM: JONATHAN T. BLANK

On Jun 15, 2020, at 11:14 PM

To: BK

I like that phrase. I like it a lot.

The last ten days have me focused on my Virginia Henrico County K-12 experience.

Your thesis is evidenced by disturbing truths.

THOSE TRUTHS NOT ONLY INCLUDE THE ABSENCE OF THE CONTRIBUTIONS OF PEOPLE OF COLOR AND THOSE ON THE MARGINS BUT OVERT SYMBOLISM AND LIES TO INDOCTRINATE AND CONTINUE OPPRESSION.

As educated as I think I am, as much as I hope I am, as you refer, one of those people, I look back now and am disturbed at how comfortable everyone including me (one of the valedictorian speakers) was with that system.

I AM DISTURBED AT HOW COMFORTABLE PEOPLE STILL ARE.

AND I HAD NO IDEA HOW IGNORANT I WAS AND IN MANY WAYS, STILL AM.

PS1-I am going to start carrying around a golf tee to serve as a conscious reminder of my own ignorance and learning curve.

06.15.2020

The golf tee Blank mentions refers to a response to Fulton's *'Divine Puzzle of Life . . .'* op-ed, which had become something of an online gathering place for viewers to expand Fulton's message. Many commenters noted inventions, art, theories, and other creations by people of African descent whose contributions have been deliberately suppressed in our history books and lessons.

The golf tee is just one such invention, dreamed up by George Franklin Grant, who also happened to be the first African-American professor at Harvard University and a dentist. In 1899 Dr. Grant—the son of former slaves— patented his design for the wooden golf tee. Prior to his invention, golfers carried buckets of sand with them from hole to hole, building small mounds from which to hit their ball.

AS A NOD TO GRANT—AND TO HIS OWN AWAKENING TO THE SYSTEMIC WHITEWASHING OF AMERICAN HISTORY— **BLANK, AN AVID GOLFER HIMSELF, BEGINS TO CARRY A GOLF TEE IN HIS POCKET AS A DAILY REMINDER OF ALL THE ANTI-RACISM WORK LEFT TO BE DONE IN THE UNITED STATES.**

AND SO, THIS IS WHERE THE TALE OF THE TEE REALLY BEGINS.

BK FULTON • JONATHAN BLANK

06.16.2020

FROM: BK FULTON

Sent: Tuesday, June 16, 2020 12:03 AM
To: Blank, Jonathan T.
Cc: Stone, Jacquelyn E.
Subject: Re: Two things

THANK YOU FOR SHARING. I WILL CARRY ONE TOO.

We are Brothers all. Your burden is mine and mine is yours. I pray that we pay the lessons forward. I am most impressed with your willingness to challenge long-held views. It is not for the faint of heart.

OUR FRAME OF THE WORLD IS ALMOST AS SACRED AS OUR FAITH. IT IS WHAT WE LEAN ON FOR UNDERSTANDING. TO QUESTION THAT UNDERSTANDING WHEN FACED WITH COMPELLING FACTS IS A COURAGEOUS ACT OF LOVE.

Only the foolish and the brave take leaps of faith. The wise know that life is a comedy and the universe is friendly. So we dance into the unknown. If we forget, we will have our tee; Brothers in the journey ... you and me.

Be Well,
BK

06.17.2020 - 06.19.2020

FROM: **JONATHAN T. BLANK**

Sent: June 17, 2020 at 12:48 AM

I GLADLY JOIN THE JOURNEY.

Jonathan T. Blank
McGuireWoods LLP

FROM: **BK FULTON**

Sent: Wednesday, June 17, 2020 2:15 AM
To: Blank, Jonathan T.
Subject: Re: Two things

WELCOME

BK

FROM: **JONATHAN T. BLANK**

On Jun 19, 2020, at 12:51 AM

I submitted this a few hours before I sent my email to Jackie and our email exchanges started. It was printed today. I wanted to share it with you. Had it been a day later it would have included a sentence about curriculum. Still carrying my tee.

Jonathan

LETTER TO THE EDITOR:

CONFEDERATE SYMBOLS MUST GO AT FREEMAN HIGH SCHOOL

From 1984 to 1988, I served as Douglas Southall Freeman (DSF) High School class president. Recently, an alumna asked me to look at my yearbook. I saw the Confederate flag, nickname and mascot, and these disturbed me. The symbols were so ingrained that the back cover included a photo of me and my classmates cheering behind a Confederate flag at a football game. My present-day self questions why we looked so comfortable.

During high school, I heard no one question those symbols. I heard no one question when our African-American classmate was handed a Confederate flag and asked to wave it while "Dixie" played. I heard no one ask how my African-American classmates and their families felt when confronted with Freeman's name, colors and history. How could we have forced those symbols on our African-American homecoming princess, treasurer, classmates,

vice principal and coaches? How do those symbols make them and today's students feel now? Those symbols cannot be rewritten to be something they are not. We loved our school and were taught to love those symbols. One was right, and the other was wrong.

SIMPLY PUT, WE WERE WRONG.
SAYING THOSE WORDS DOES NOT CHANGE OUR PAST. BUT I HOPE IT STARTS A HEALING PROCESS WHERE HISTORY IS TRUTHFULLY TOLD AND STUDENTS ARE NOT INDOCTRINATED, INDIRECTLY OR DIRECTLY, TO CELEBRATE THE CONFEDERACY.

I hope it starts a process to delink Freeman's name, nickname and colors so that they are retired like the school's mascot, Confederate flag and "Dixie."

Saying we were wrong and removing Freeman's glorified Confederate past will not cure the wrongs. However, these actions could create real change, like that proposed in a petition started by recent graduates. Like removing Confederate statues, removing Freeman's Confederate symbols could say to African-American classmates and school personnel that they matter; that Black Lives Matter. It is a start.

Originally published on https://www.richmond.com/opinion

FROM: BK FULTON

Subject: Re: Sharing more of the journey and the tee
Date: June 19, 2020 at 3:26:16 AM EDT
To: Jonathan Blank   Cc: Stone, Jacquelyn E.

Very interesting and timely. Your piece is honest. Thank you for walking in that truth. I would like us to do a call today just because. Ironically, I wrote a piece on truth, love and change on Saturday and it was picked up locally and nationally on Sunday and Wednesday respectively. The Jewish community has been integral to my life for a very long time. My kids were adopted from the Jewish Child Care Association in NYC; my mentor in law school was Jewish; a photo of a Jewish scholar and his African-American students hangs in my office; the man who recruited me into Verizon was Jewish; and now in retirement, my movie mentor is Jewish. I am "part" Jewish.

YOUR PIECE AND MY PIECE MAKES US BOTH ESSENTIAL PARTS OF THE DIVINE PUZZLE OF LIFE.

THERE WILL BE NO TRUE PEACE IN THE WORLD UNTIL WE EACH BRING OUR PIECE TO THE WORLD. THE TRUTH OF OUR LIVES COLLECTIVELY AS HUMAN BEINGS ALWAYS RESOLVES AS LOVE.

I TOO CARRY MY TEE.

See my op-ed, *The Divine Puzzle of Life as Seen by a Native Son of Virginia*, republished on mariashriver.com.

BK

Original painted steel artwork by Jewish artist Patricia Govezensky from Tel Aviv. We own the original. We won it at auction the day my op-ed above was published. God is in the details. Let's do something together at the JCC [Jewish Community Center]. We can show my da Vinci speech, read our articles and do a Q&A. It will be healing. Let's make it so. **GOD PUT US TOGETHER FOR SOME REASON. MAY WE SEE IT THROUGH. SHALOM.**

ON JULY 1, 2020, THE MONUMENT TO CONFEDERATE GENERAL STONEWALL JACKSON WAS THE FIRST TO BE TAKEN DOWN FROM RICHMOND'S MONUMENT AVENUE, WITH OTHERS TO FOLLOW.

JB'S REMARKS AT THE MCGUIREWOODS TOWN HALL

On June 12, 2020, McGuireWoods Chairman Jonathan Harmon, the only African American to lead an Am Law 100 law firm, had an op-ed piece published in the Wall Street Journal titled: *"My Father's Advice: 'Don't Hate, Don't Hide, Don't be a Victim."* On June 22, 2020, Chairman Harmon led his firm's first firmwide Town Hall on Racial Equality and Justice. A panel was convened of two African-American partners, three African-American associates, the Chief Operating Officer who is African American and two non-African-American partners. Jonathan Blank was one of the two non-African-American partners.

Chairman Harmon invited his entire firm to join in the discussion. Jonathan Harmon and Jonathan Blank started at McGuireWoods on the same day as summer associates and practiced together since their first days as associates. Jonathan Blank was honored to join the panel and was presented with the third question by Chairman Harmon.

THE QUESTION WAS: DO YOU HAVE DIFFICULTY OR HAVE YOU HAD DIFFICULTY HAVING DISCUSSIONS WITH AFRICAN AMERICANS ABOUT RACE?

THE TALE OF THE TEE

JONATHAN BLANK'S RESPONSE IS CAPTURED, IN PART, BELOW:

I will start with a non-answer but will hopefully get to an answer. I talked to a number of younger people in the firm who think we are just checking the box, we are just having this Town Hall to look good. I talked to older people who said that you just put Blank on there because he is left of center liberal. It does not matter if we are young, old, Republican or Democrat, right, left; we are family. You talk to family members about things that are uncomfortable.

SO, THE ANSWER TO THE QUESTION IS OF COURSE, IT IS UNCOMFORTABLE TALKING ABOUT SOMETHING THAT YOU ARE NOT SURE OF, YOU DON'T UNDERSTAND, AND WHERE YOU DON'T WALK IN THE SAME SHOES.

Clearly I haven't been racially profiled. It is hard for me to have that conversation but if not us, as part of family, then who? If not now, when? We have got to get past comfortability and seize on the opportunity for real change. It can't be as a white person, "Well I have a black friend." It can't be that "my Chairman is black". It can't be that "the Rector of the University I attended was black." It can't be that "my firm had an African-American hiring partner." It can't be "I am not a racist."

WE HAVE TO GO INTO THESE CONVERSATIONS VULNERABLE AND WHEN I SAY WE, I AM INCLUDING ME. BUT WE HAVE TO BE PREPARED.

As a lawyer, we read the law all the time. We google. We can ask our African-American colleagues and friends, but darn it go prepare yourself, go research, go investigate. We spend so much time on other things but we don't spend time on this issue. We need to spend, as family, more time researching, learning, introspection. We have to do it. We have to be prepared to listen. When we do, I think, at least when I have done it, with you, with others..., I have been rewarded many times moreover than the uncomfortableness of the conversation.

SO TO THOSE WHO SAY WE ARE CHECKING THE BOX. I DON'T THINK WE ARE CHECKING THE BOX.

I THINK WE ARE STARTING A VERY DIFFICULT CONVERSATION THAT HAS TO CONTINUE.

YOU HAVE TO BE VULNERABLE, YOU HAVE TO PUT YOURSELF OUT THERE.

OTHERWISE, THE LAST 50 YEARS ARE GOING TO BE LIKE THE LAST 500 YEARS, THE LAST 5000 YEARS AND WE ARE NOT GOING TO BE ABLE TO ATTACK RACISM.

CONCLUSION

THROUGH THIS EXCHANGE, BOTH BLANK AND FULTON BEGAN CARRYING A GOLF TEE IN THEIR POCKET EVERY DAY—A SUBTLE REMINDER OF THE RESPONSIBILITY BOTH MEN HAVE TAKEN ON, BENDING THAT MORAL ARC OF THE UNIVERSE DEEPER TOWARDS JUSTICE.

From that original act of thoughtful responsibility—Stone and her colleagues cleaning graffiti off the Oliver Hill historical marker—to the conversation and subsequent collaboration that followed, this story is just one microcosm of what is happening, and what needs to continue happening across the United States and around the globe, if we want to reconstruct a culture, a society, a country, a world in which all people are equal, recognized for their value and contributions, and can aspire to achieve anything.

WE ALL MUST LEAN INTO LOVE FOR OUR CHILDREN AND THEIR CHILDREN.

WE NEED TO BE ABLE TO TALK TO EACH OTHER, TO TELL OUR STORIES. IF WE BEGIN THIS WORK OF HEALING FROM A PLACE WHERE WE CAN'T EVEN TALK TO EACH OTHER, WE WON'T GET ANYWHERE.

Over the span of a week, Blank and Fulton shared their stories and points of view authentically and with open minds and hearts. One man is African American, the other is Jewish. The custom golf tee they are having made as a symbol of their shared commitment to the work ahead was created by a man of Lebanese descent. On either side of the tee are engraved initials: "BK" (symbolizing "be kind") and "JB" (for "just believe"). The tee is made from the jawbone of a donkey to symbolize strength coupled with the ability to win against the odds and rare metals symbolizing the precious value of humanity.

THE 'TALE OF THE TEE' REPRESENTS THE KIND OF HEALING DIALOGUE THAT ALL OF US CAN HAVE, SHOULD HAVE, TO PERFECT OUR MORE PERFECT UNION.

Put simply, the authors ask readers to remember to be kind and just believe. The moral arc will allow us to use truth to help us resolve the divine puzzle of life. It always resolves to love.

BK Fulton

Jonathan Blank

ABOUT BK & JONATHAN

BK FULTON,

BK was born in Hampton, VA to Flora and Bennie Fulton. He has two sisters, Shauna Fulton and DeVora Brookes. BK is the founding Chairman & CEO of Soulidifly Productions, a feature film and media investment company designed to promote a more inclusive narrative in contemporary media. Soulidifly is the first independent film company to produce four feature films in their first year of business (*River Runs Red, Atone, 1 Angry Black Man,* and *Love Dot Com: The Social Experiment*). BK is also the author of the popular *Mr. Business: The Adventures of Little BK* children's book series and founder of *SoulVision Magazine* and *SoulVision.TV*. Prior to becoming a full-time author and media entrepreneur, BK was Vice President of the Mid-Atlantic Region (VA, MD, DC, DE) for Verizon Communications, Inc. and President of Verizon Virginia and West Virginia. He has also held senior leadership, media, technology and policy development posts with the U.S. Department of Commerce, AOL, Time Warner and the National Urban League. BK is a *ComputerWorld Smithsonian Laureate Medal* recipient, and his thought-leading papers on technology and community building are permanently archived at the Smithsonian Institute. He holds a Bachelor's degree from Virginia Tech, a Master of Science degree and Sloan Fellowship from Harvard's - Kennedy School of Government and the New School's - Milano School of Management and Policy Analysis, and a Juris Doctorate from New York Law School. BK is the father of twin boys (Joshua and Terrell) and is married to Jacquelyn E. Stone, Esq.

JONATHAN BLANK

Jonathan was born in Richmond, VA to Rhona and Irving Blank. Since 1995, Blank has practiced law with McGuireWoods from its Richmond, Baltimore and Charlottesville offices. His national commercial practice concentrates on energy law with a special interest in alternative energy. From 2018 to present, he has served as the international and national Chairman of the firm's Business and Securities Litigation Department. Blank's pro bono practice has included co-leading America's seminal human trafficking case, Virginia's repeal of automatic suspension of licenses for failure to pay court costs and fines, and a number of Innocence Project cases. Blank worked for Governor L. Douglas Wilder's speechwriters and policy directors team, was appointed by Governor Mark Warner to serve on Virginia's Motor Vehicle Dealer Board, and was appointed by Governor Timothy Kaine to serve on Virginia's Board of Corrections. Blank served as the Charlottesville Democratic Party Chairman from 2008 to 2010. He also was President of the Virginia's Legal Aid Justice Center, where he continues to serve on its Board. Jonathan and his wife, Dr. Susan Blank, have two sets of twin daughters — Madeline and Alexandra, and Caroline and Isabel.

CPSIA information can be obtained
at www.ICGtesting.com
Printed in the USA
BVHW020924010920
587179BV00047B/204